Moka Shares

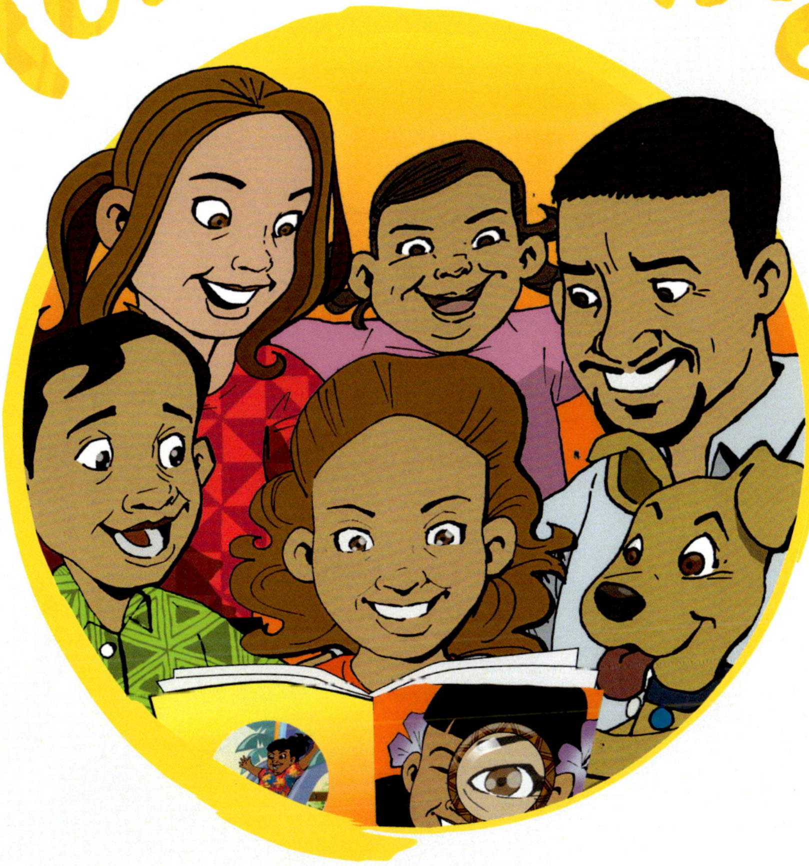

DAHLIA MALAEULU

illustrations by
Darcy Solia

Moka loves to share ...

with everyone, every day!

On **Aho Gofua**,
Moka shares her breakfast.

On **Aho Ua**,
Moka shares her umbrella.

On **Aho Lotu**,
Moka shares her toys.

On **Aho Tuloto**,
Moka shares her book.

On **Aho Falaile**,
Moka shares her blanket.

On **Aho Faiumu,**
Moka shares her song.

On **Aho Tapu**,
the last day of the week ...

Everyone shares
something with Moka ...
because she shared
something with everyone!

Glossary

Aho Gofua	Monday
Aho Ua	Tuesday
Aho Lotu	Wednesday
Aho Tuloto	Thursday
Aho Falaile	Friday
Aho Faiumu	Saturday
Aho Tapu	Sunday

Pronunciation Guide

Short Vowel Sounds

a	ah	as in c**u**p
e	eh	as in b**e**d
i	ee	as in **e**at
o	o	as in **o**r
u	oo	as in t**o**

Long Vowel Sounds

ā	as in f**a**r
ē	as in **e**gg
ī	as in m**ee**t
ō	as in th**ough**t
ū	as in l**oo**t

Extra Notes

When the letter ‘t’ is followed by the letter ‘e’ or ‘i’ it is pronounced as an ‘s’, for example:

titipi (knife) is pronunced as sisipi
tele (kick) is pronunced as sele

But transliteral words from English to Vagahau Niue do not have the ‘s’ sound for example:

teti pea - teddy bear
kapati - cupboard

Consonants

f	fa	as in **f**at
g	nga	as in si**ng**er
h	ha	as in **h**at
k	ka	as in **g**et
l	la	as in **l**ive
m	ma	as in **m**en
n	na	as in **n**ote
p	pa	as in **p**ad
r	ra	as in **r**ah
s	sa	as in **s**it
t	ta	as in **d**art (combined t/d sound)
v	va	as in **v**ery

Mila's
My Pasifika Series

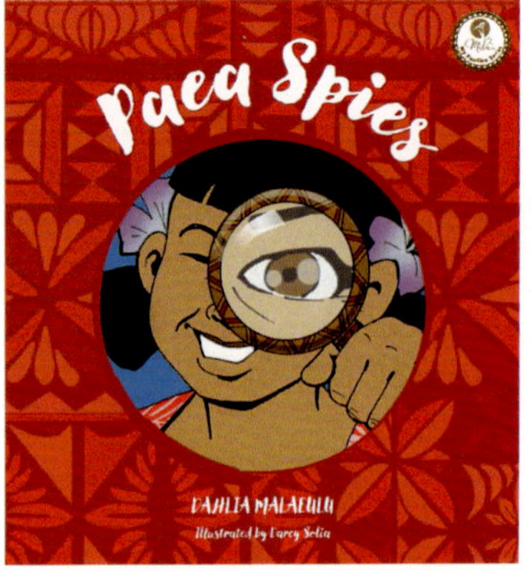
Paea Spies
DAHLIA MALAEULU
Illustrated by Darcy Solia

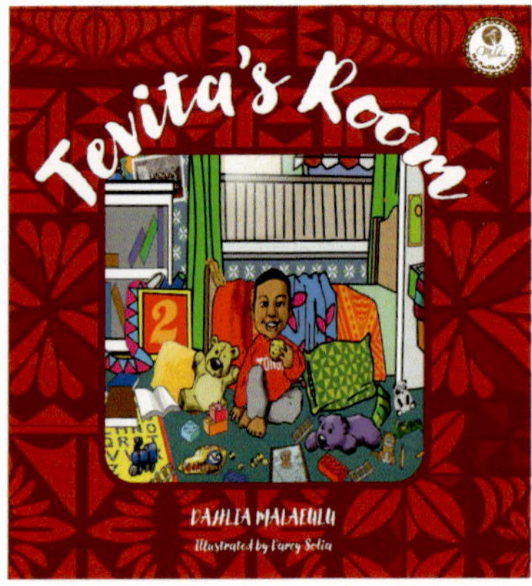
Tevita's Room
DAHLIA MALAEULU
Illustrated by Darcy Solia

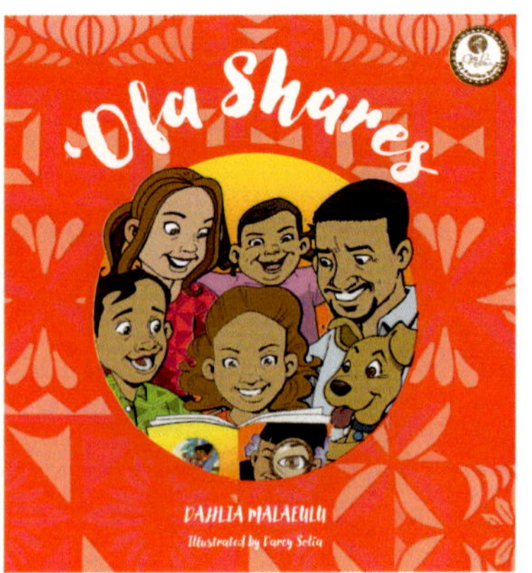
'Ofa Shares
DAHLIA MALAEULU
Illustrated by Darcy Solia

Mele Spies
DAHLIA MALAEULU
Illustrated by Darcy Solia

Tule's Room
DAHLIA MALAEULU
Illustrated by Darcy Solia

Moka Shares
DAHLIA MALAEULU
Illustrated by Darcy Solia

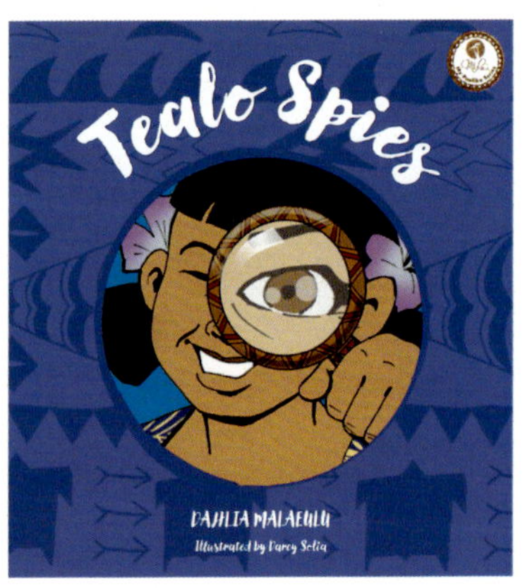
Tealo Spies
DAHLIA MALAEULU
Illustrated by Darcy Solia

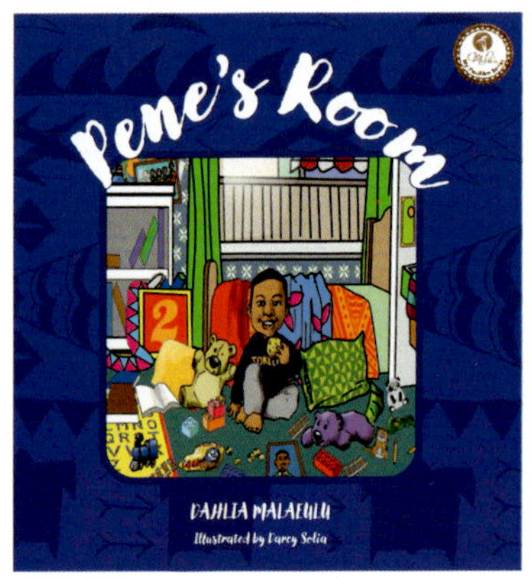
Pene's Room
DAHLIA MALAEULU
Illustrated by Darcy Solia

Hui Shares
DAHLIA MALAEULU
Illustrated by Darcy Solia

Mila's

Lagi Spies
Dahlia Malaeulu

Mase's Room
Dahlia Malaeulu
Illustrated by Darcy Solia

Malia Shares
Dahlia Malaeulu
Illustrated by Darcy Solia

LOSI THE GIANT FISHERMAN
By Dahlia Malaeulu
Samoan Myths and Legends Pick a Path Collection

Fale Sāmoa
Dahlia Malaeulu
Illustrated by Darcy Solia

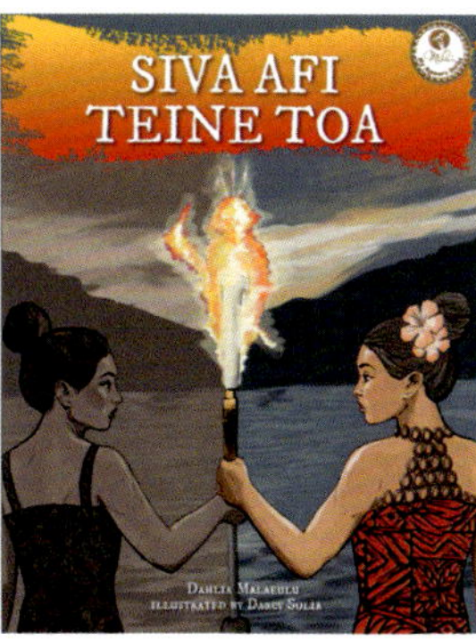
SIVA AFI TEINE TOA
Dahlia Malaeulu
Illustrated by Darcy Solia

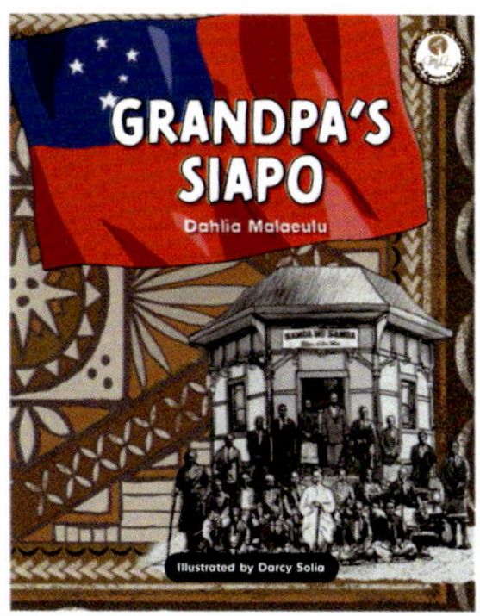
GRANDPA'S SIAPO
Dahlia Malaeulu
Illustrated by Darcy Solia

Tama Sāmoa
DAHLIA & MANI MALAEULU

DAHLIA MALAEULU
Teine Sāmoa

A NEW DAWN
EMELI SIONE

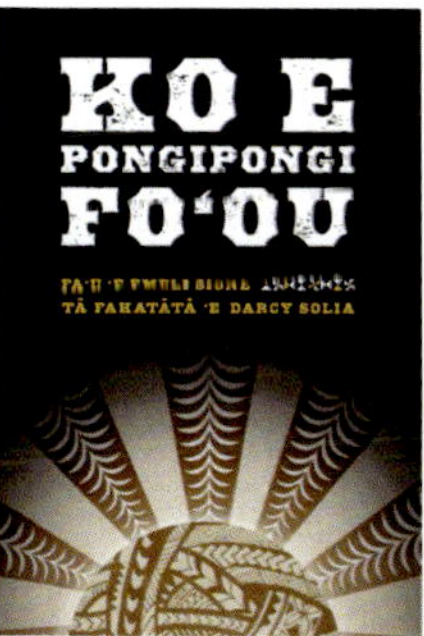
KO E PONGIPONGI FOʻOU
TĀ FAKATĀTĀ ʻE DARCY SOLIA

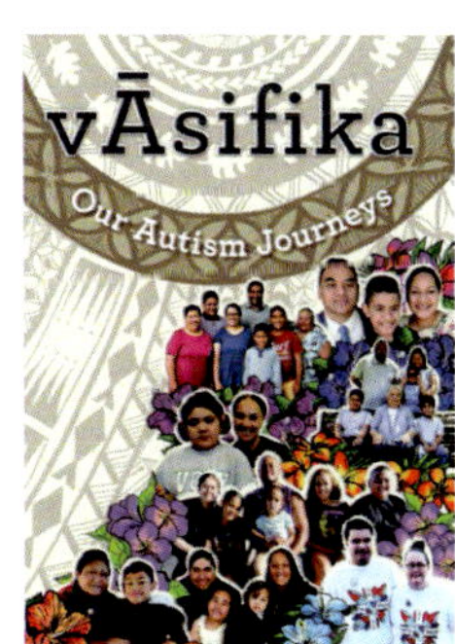
vĀsifika
Our Autism Journeys

PASIFIKA NAVIGATORS
Pasifika Student Poetry Collection

Tama Pasifika Wellbeing Journal
CONNECT
TALANOA
HEAL

Teine Pasifika Wellbeing Journal
SEEN
HEARD
VALUED

I am Pasifika Wellbeing Journal

Published by Mila's Books
www.milabooks.com

A catalogue record for this book is available from the National Library of New Zealand.

ISBN 978 1 7386061 6 0

Original story written by Dahlia Malaeulu
Translated by Inangaro Vakaafi
Illustrated by Darcy Solia
Designed by Liz Tui Morris
Edited by Emeli Sione

Recipient of a 2022 Contestable Fund Grant
from Copyright Licensing New Zealand